HOW TO GET ENRICH OUT OF THE
DEBT CYCLE

HOW TO GET ENRICH OUT OF THE
DEBT CYCLE

HENNIE REYNDERS

authorHOUSE®

AuthorHouse™ UK Ltd.
1663 Liberty Drive
Bloomington, IN 47403 USA
www.authorhouse.co.uk
Phone: 0800.197.4150

Published by AuthorHouse 12/09/2013

ISBN: 978-1-4918-8783-7 (sc)
ISBN: 978-1-4918-8784-4 (e)

CONTENTS

CHAPTER 1

ABOUT MONEY

There are four things every person has more of
than they know: sins, debt, years and foes.
—Persian proverb

How to manage money is probably something you need to learn from your parents, the same way they taught you proper manners. Unfortunately, it is often in those early days of one's upbringing that things start going wrong. Parents want to give their children nothing but the best and will go to extremes to give their children what they ask, even if they know this is a waste of money.

Having money often turns into a matter of competition. If I have more money than you, then I am in a much better position than you. In fact, I may even be a much better person. The idea that money makes you a quality person is as totally wrong as it is common; the amount of money in your purse or your bank balance definitely does not determine your integrity or character.

We often believe that celebrities or rich people are the happiest people in the world. But just read the daily or weekly papers and magazines, and you will realise than many of them are not happy at all. Happiness is a state of mind.

There are two major principles that you need to understand, even though on the surface neither of them appears to have anything to do with money management.

The first is that *there is no correlation between money and happiness in the long term*. Permanent happiness can never be found in worldly things. As the coach said to the team in the film Cool Running: "If you don't have enough without the gold medal, you will not have enough with the gold medal".

> *1 John 2:15-17 Do not love the world nor the things in the world. If anyone loves the world, the love of the Father is not in him. For all that is in the world, the lust of the flesh and the lust of the eyes and the boastful pride of life, is not from the Father, but is from the world. The world is passing away, and also its lusts; but the one who does the will of God lives forever.*

The second principle—and this is one of the laws of nature which will never change—is that *what you sow, you will reap*. If you spend/invest (sow) your money on worthless items, you will earn/inherit (reap) nothing. It is like a child buying himself a simple plastic toy which lasts for five minutes compared with a child who builds himself a toy (say a wire car) which he can play with for years and, in most cases, costs him nothing more than the time he spent building it.

> *Debts are like children: the smaller they are,*
> *the more noise they make.*
> —Spanish proverb

> *Before borrowing money from a friend, decide*
> *which you need most.*
> —American proverb

Life is all about choices, and the same applies to money. You have a choice how you are going to spend that next rand. I want to help you with those choices.

> ***Ecclesiastes 5:10*** *Whoever loves money never has enough; whoever loves wealth is never satisfied with their income. This too is meaningless.*

The question is; where do we start? Perhaps you are reading this book because you don't have any money problems and you simply want to learn how to spend your money wisely, which will make it much easier to make wise choices in future. But I don't think that is the case. It is more likely that you are reading this book because you do have money problems and you want to find ways to get out of a sticky financial situation. The way out is probably going to be a tough one that will take time and demand dedication, but in the end you will find that happiness again.

As you read this book, you will realise where you made mistakes. You will also discover what is needed to solve these problems.

Credit is a bit like a hangover. As Joyce Brothers put it:

> *Credit buying is much like being drunk. The buzz happens immediately and gives you a lift . . . . The hangover comes the day after.*

This is all well and good, but you still have to live your life and be able to apply the principles of money management. Do you really know how? If the stove plate is on and hot and you put your hand on it, it will burn you. Likewise, as long as you live, you will need money to stay alive; if you spend your money on the wrongs things or do not use your money wisely, you will get burnt.

This is the message I want to bring home to you right from the start: when you spend your money, do it wisely. Now, how would a wise man spend his money? Do I spend my money in order to compete with others, to show off—or do I base my decisions on the need to provide for myself or my family on the basis of what I can afford?

You must get into the habit of always asking yourself:

What would the wise man do?

In human society, we will find people living at different material levels, and that is simply natural. Through the eyes of God we are all equal, and that is spiritual thing. Here on earth we have to play a certain role, we have a purpose, and we have to find that purpose. When we do, life makes sense.

> ***1 Timothy 6:17-19*** *Instruct those who are rich in this present world not to be conceited or to fix their hope on the uncertainty of riches, but on God, who richly supplies us with all things to enjoy. Instruct them to do good, to be rich in good works, to be generous and ready to share, storing up for themselves the treasure of a good foundation for the future, so that they may take hold of that which is life indeed.*

The fact is: you are currently living at a certain *level* in society and you have a *role* to play. Your level in society will be determined by your income and the position you hold. Your role, on the other hand, will be determined by your insight and ability to act like a wise man; it will be based more on the spiritual and the ability to understand the law of nature (wisdom).

> ***Luke 16:14*** *The Pharisees, who loved money, heard all this and were sneering at Jesus He said to them, "You are the ones who justify yourselves in the eyes of others, but God knows your hearts. What people value highly is detestable in God's sight."*

Money often brings out man's evil side, and that is greed. Greed is constantly wanting to have more. We tend to accuse the rich of being stingy and/or greedy, but actually the urge to have more than someone else can be found at all levels of society. The opposite of greediness is being content with what you have. If you spend more money than you can afford at your level, are you not being greedy?

> *Luke 12:15* *Then he said to them, "Watch out! Be on your guard against all kinds of greed; a man's life does not consist in the abundance of his possessions."*

There are many economists who say the credit crunch in 2008 was solely due to greed. Later in my book I will explain how nations are going down because of greed. We are currently seeing how America is being replaced by China as having the world's largest economy, and the predictions are that China will be number 1 by 2020—if not sooner.

If this is what a nation can become, how easily can it happen with a private household?

We must understand the rules of the money management game. I will explain to you in this book all the concepts, principles and rules of money management, but you must understand that these concepts will never be effective if you don't apply them with your heart and your mind. The moment you do not spend money in accordance with your level or role, but because you want to impress your neighbours, you are dead in the water.

> *1 Peter 5:2* *Be shepherds of God's flock that is under your care, serving as overseers—not because you must, but because you are willing, as God wants you to be; not greedy for money, but eager to serve;*

What is credit (debt)?

The simplest definition of credit is that it is the amount of money you owe somebody else.

The bigger question we must ask is why you want this credit in the first instance: Why do I owe somebody else money?

The obvious answer to this question is that I borrowed money from the person or institution in order to buy something, or I bought something from this person or business on credit.

You need something which you can't afford to buy cash, so you apply for credit. Let's define 'need'. If you are going to buy something on credit, you must first of all define it based on your level and role as explained above. Do I buy this because it is really essential for me to have it?

> **Proverbs 22:7** *The rich rules over the poor, and the borrower is the slave of the lender.*

Money itself is not evil at all, and there's nothing wrong with having a lot of money.

> *1 **Timothy 6:6-12** But godliness with contentment is great gain. For we brought nothing into the world, and we can take nothing out of it. But if we have food and clothing, we will be content with that. People who want to get rich fall into temptation and a trap and into many foolish and harmful desires that plunge men into ruin and destruction. For*

*the love of money is a root of all kinds of evil.
Some people, eager for money, have wandered
from the faith and pierced themselves with
many griefs. But you, man of God, flee from
all this, and pursue righteousness, godliness,
faith, love, endurance and gentleness. Fight
the good fight of the faith. Take hold of the
eternal life to which you were called when you
made your good confession in the presence of
many witnesses.*

Clearly, *"flee from all this, and pursue righteousness,
godliness, faith, love, endurance and gentleness"*, means
that you must not regard money as a goal. The goal is the
pursuit of righteousness, godliness etc., whether you are
rich or poor. You need money because you have to feed
your family or want to do more for them, for example give
them a better than average house or a holiday. Money is
just a tool or an instrument, like a screwdriver, drill or
knife. You can use it or abuse it. Almost anything can be
put to good use or bad; it depends entirely on the user, not
on the object. Money is not an end, but a means, a medium
of exchange, an instrument.

*1 Timothy 6:17-19. "Command those who are
rich in this present world not to be arrogant
nor to put their hope in wealth, which is so
uncertain, but to put their hope in God, who
richly provides us with everything for our
enjoyment. Command them to do good, to be
rich in good deeds, and to be generous and
willing to share. In this way they will lay up
treasure for themselves as a firm foundation*

for the coming age, so that they may take hold
of the life that is truly life.

If you lose your value system—integrity, honesty etc.—then you become useless to society. Money might buy you a place on earth, even if you have lost your value system, but definitely not in heaven. The balance in your bank account or in your pocket definitely doesn't determine your integrity or honesty.

When you see how people deal with it, you might think debt is something entirely new to mankind. Yet people have been getting into debt even in the Stone Age. Dr Michael Hudson, in an article 'The new economic archaeology of debt', refers to a statement made by Fritz Heichelheim: "Around 5000 BC dates, olives, figs, nuts, or seeds of grain were probably lent out to serfs, poorer farmers, and dependants to sow and plant, and naturally an increased portion of the harvest had to be returned in kind. Naturally! In addition to fruits and seeds, animals could be borrowed too for a fixed time limit, the loan being repaid according to a fixed percentage from the young animals born subsequently." Farmers everywhere still do this today: they take out a loan (or get credit), which has to be paid back in accordance with a certain agreement.

What happened in those days if you did not pay back the loan? According to Dr Hudson, in ancient Mesopotamia there was a rule between the two parties that if the loan was not repaid as agreed, the borrower would forfeit moveable property, especially livestock, women and children, or would have to repay with his own labour or service.

In the kingdom of Babylonia you could be used as a slave if you didn't pay back your debt. And that was about 8000 years ago.

> *Proverbs 22:7, NIV. "You are not really free when you are in debt. The rich rule over the poor, and the borrower is servant to the lender."*

Babylon, which many historians describe as the richest city in the world, was a kingdom of many firsts—the first engineers, the first astronomers, the first mathematicians, the first financiers and the first written language. Why do I refer back to these ancient times? I would like to explain that what you are experiencing is not something new. Debt and the issues around it go back to even before the barter trade, when there was no money and people simply swapped goods for other goods. I will share stories with you from those times, such as what the meaning of the sound of money is and why you have to pay yourself first. I will repeat the advice from the richest of the rich from that time—and believe me, the same principles are still true today.

In a sense, modern civilization already existed in those days. People were living in a rich world, but they got greedy and believed they controlled everything—and then they lost it all.

> **Proverbs 23:4-5** *Do not wear yourself out to get rich; do not trust your own cleverness. Cast but a glance at riches, and they are gone, for they will surely sprout wings and fly off to the sky like an eagle.*

James 5:1-6. Now listen, you rich people, weep and wail because of the misery that is coming on you. Your wealth has rotted, and moths have eaten your clothes. Your gold and silver are corroded. Their corrosion will testify against you and eat your flesh like fire. You have hoarded wealth in the last days. Look! The wages you failed to pay the workers who mowed your fields are crying out against you. The cries of the harvesters have reached the ears of the Lord Almighty. You have lived on earth in luxury and self-indulgence. You have fattened yourselves in the day of slaughter. You have condemned and murdered the innocent one, who was not opposing you.

Proverbs 11:28 He who trusts in his riches will fall, but the righteous shall flourish as the green leaf.

I must emphasise that it was not "riches" that led to their downfall, but the fact that they were not righteous. I constantly see how friends and colleagues change when they get promotion, a higher income or inherit a large amount of money. They change and they don't even realise it, and the remarks and guidance from an old friend are simply disregarded.

CHAPTER 2

WHY DO YOU WANT CREDIT?

People have an endless number of reasons why they need credit. Just ask the lady whether she really needed that pair of shoes or that handbag. Ask the gentlemen talking to a motor vehicle salesman whether he really has to have that car he is about to buy.

Every day, consumers are confronted with advertisements which focus on their psychological weaknesses. Such advertisements 'manufacture' a need for an item the consumer doesn't actually need. They persuade the customer that he must have it, otherwise he will be shunned by his peer group and will be seen as somebody with no vision. They tell him that he has to "keep up with the Joneses". But of course, by definition the Joneses always have more, no matter how much you have. Marketing campaigns force the consumer to buy something he doesn't need and, in most cases, does not have the money for either.

Sure, everybody dreams of possessing a (better) house, a (better) car or (even more) beautiful clothes. You can add to that list forever: a holiday at the seaside, or even overseas, or—even better—a holiday home at the sea. You may dream, and in fact you must dream; but you must *do something* before you can have any of these things. Dreaming is one thing; making your dream come true is something else. You may dream, but you should keep your perspective. Remember the level I mentioned earlier: you must determine your ability to pay back your debt.

> *Romans 13:5-7. Therefore one must be in subjection, not only to avoid God's wrath but also for the sake of conscience. For because of this you also pay taxes, for the authorities are ministers of God, attending to this very thing. Pay to all what is owed to them: taxes to whom taxes are owed, revenue to whom revenue is owed, respect to whom respect is owed, honour to whom honour is owed.*

> *Numbers 30:2. If a man vows a vow to the Lord, or swears an oath to bind himself by a pledge, he shall not break his word. He shall do according to all that proceeds out of his mouth.*

Now buying the item you have in mind is not the first step you must take. The first thing to do is to ask: Can I afford it? This is a matter of how large your income is. You have to determine how much money is available to buy the item you want. You must budget for this item. We will discuss budgeting in more detail later on.

When you decide to take up a loan or buy something on credit, you need to remember you must repay it. Why must you repay it? This aspect is related to integrity or, as Mr Barack Obama put it in his inaugural speech as president of America, "he expects fair play". What else is fair play than obeying the rules of the game, the clauses of a contract or the content of an agreement, either in writing or verbally? If you have made a promise, shouldn't you abide by it? What would you do if somebody didn't keep the agreement you made with him? In the book "The 8th Habit", by Stephen R. Covey, he referred to a survey done in America in which certain questions were put to thousands of people across cultures, religions, philosophies and companies. The number one behaviour people expected from their colleagues, friends, family members or boss/manager was "integrity". When you are called to account, will you be able to say with a clear conscience that you played fair, you didn't cheat, you didn't go offside? How many times we find that the supporters of a soccer or rugby team go ballistic because the referee didn't see the opponent was offside when he scored a goal? Such a goal is disallowed because it is not fair play. In the chapter on the recovery plan we will come back to this topic.

> *Psalm 37:21 ESV. The wicked borrows but does not pay back, but the righteous is generous and gives;*

> *Proverbs 3:27-28 ESV. Do not withhold good from those to whom it is due, when it is in your power to do it. Do not say to your neighbour, "Go, and come again, tomorrow I will give it"—when you have it with you.*

Credit can be a friend or a foe that you invite into your house. Credit gives you this wonderful opportunity to obtain something which you currently can't afford, but are willing and committed to pay off in instalments over a period of time.

Credit will become part of your life, it will be a family member and certainly it will be a demanding partner or shareholder of your estate. You are at risk of losing your family assets, in other words you put your family's assets at risk with your decisions.

Before you invite Mr Credit into your life, you must be quite sure that you would like to have him on your team. Do you really need him? Before you answer yes, let's first of all ask ourselves what Mr Credit's behaviour is like.

Mr Credit will expect you—:

- to pay him first of all;
- to pay him consistently every month;
- to pay the full instalment every month;
- to pay him interest on the outstanding amount;
- to pay him some administration fees;
- not go conclude other credit agreements which may put the relationship with your current creditors in jeopardy;
- to make arrangements well in advance if you can't pay an instalment;
- to keep to the arrangement you made with him;.
- to understand that if you don't pay him, he will have the authority to take legal steps against you;

- to understand that he can take full control of your income and decide, in his sole discretion, how it must be spent.

If you don't honour the above commitments, he (Mr Credit) will take full control of your estate.

> *Matthew 18:25 Since he was not able to pay, the master ordered that he and his wife and his children and all that he had be sold to repay the debt.*

You will be in a "financial jail". You will work for a salary. but other people will decide how it must be distributed among your creditors and what you can afford. There will be no financial freedom, and for years to come you will have no say in your spending patterns. Isn't this pure slavery? When you start with credit, you become the slave of the person to whom you owe the money.

> *Debt is the slavery of the free.*
> *—Publilius Syrus quotes*
> *(Roman author, 1st century B.C.)*

I have seen many people who never recovered after a financial downturn in their personal finances. It takes detail planning, years of commitment and dedication to regain one's financial wellness.

Think again: Do you want to invite Mr Credit into your space? Credit can be a friend, but then you have to follow the steps that are prescribed in this book. You have to abide by the rules of the credit game!

You have to stay in control of your finances, whatever it takes!

Thank you for reading this book and for spending time with me. If you have read this far, you are serious about improving your financial life skills.

Chapter 3

CREDIT—YOUR FRIEND

In the business world they talk about "gearing". Gearing is the use of credit to put you in a better position—to produce more products and then make more profit.

Gearing is the ratio between your own capital and outside capital (credit). A hardware shop owner might realise that not all his customers have trucks, and that if he starts delivering building materials for his customers he will sell more. When he makes his calculations (draws up his budget), his projections indicate that with the additional sales he will make he will be able to buy a truck on credit and the instalment will be paid for by the additional sales he will be making, and he will even make more profit (money left after deduction expenses). Making use of outside capital puts him in a better business position. He may be able to pay off the truck in 60 months, and if he maintains his truck properly he will be able to use the truck for many years after paying off the debt.

In this case, credit is a helpful friend.

Businesses will normally make use of outside capital because it is difficult to fund everything with their own money, but the ratio must never be more than 1:1—that means R1 own capital to R1 outside (borrowed) capital. The moment you make use of more outside capital than your own, then you, the owner, are at risk, because the lender(s) can start controlling your environment.

When you are working for a salary, the approach is a little different. You are employed at a fixed salary and you only get yearly increases or bonuses, and that means you don't have the scope to increase your income like the businessman did.

The reality that you are facing is that your income is fixed, but your expenses can vary every month.

Now you have to define your lifestyle. Just sit for a moment and think of the number of different vehicles that you see standing at your workplace. The owners of those vehicles are all working for the same company. Why can one person drive a more expensive car than the other? Let us look at the possible reasons:

- Maybe the one earns more than the other.
- Maybe the one lives in a much cheaper house, but treats himself to an expensive car.
- Maybe his parents are very rich and they bought it for him.
- Maybe the other has a large amount invested in shares, unit trusts, a second property or a savings account, therefore he drives a relatively cheap vehicle.

- Maybe his/her spouse earns a very large salary and can afford to buy expensive cars.
- Maybe the owner has been working for the company for many years and can now afford to drive a better car.
- Maybe he or she is the only breadwinner of the family and therefore has to drive a very cheap vehicle.

As you can see, there are plenty of maybe's. The bottom line is, you don't know the situation in another person's home. My dad always said "Every house has its cross". You might have an idea what your neighbours and friends go through, but unless they tell you it will always be just a perception.

Your income bracket determines your living standard; your lifestyle is something you decide on. Income and standard of living need to be in sync, otherwise you're going to land in serious trouble if you start making debts which you can't afford.

You have to define your financial framework, and we call this a budget. Your budget will be your guide and will tell you what lifestyle you can afford to adopt.

If your income (salary) is R10 000 per month, then your expenses should not be more than that. You have to have the discipline to stay within the R10 000 limit and the ability to understand the priority of every expense:

- The roof over your head
- The cost of transport to and from work

- Your food
- Your clothes
- Utility accounts
- Contractual commitments

These are restrictions you can't ignore—expenses that must be paid, where you cannot miss any payment.

Anything that is alive grows, it gets bigger and stronger. Likewise, you would not like to be forced to accept a fixed standard of living year in and year out. You also want to grow, just to be better off, maybe get married, move into a bigger house, have more children, go on an overseas trip or just have a nice vacation at the sea. That is all possible, but it needs planning!

Getting credit may be the only solution to grow a business, as in the example above. The business I referred to above was able to cross the limitations set by its current income because it created a way to increase its income. You must also gear yourself to move forward, but you must do it responsibly. Whenever you explore the credit option, make sure it stays your friend.

There is an important concept that the Lord teaches us in the scriptures, and that is the concept of "abundance".

> ***Matthew 6:25, 33*** *Do not worry then, saying, 'What will we eat?' or 'What will we drink?' or 'What will we wear for clothing?' For the Gentiles eagerly seek all these things; for your heavenly Father knows that you need all these things. But seek first His kingdom and*

His righteousness, and all these things will be added to you.

We must find the Kingdom of God, but He also expects us to work:

Proverbs 6:6 ESV. Go to the ant, O sluggard; consider her ways, and be wise. Without having any chief, officer, or ruler, she prepares her bread in summer and gathers her food in harvest. How long will you lie there, O sluggard? When will you arise from your sleep? A little sleep, a little slumber, a little folding of the hands to rest,

Although God explains in the above two verses how you must live your life by living in his Kingdom and by hard work, there is something else that you will find exist in God's creation, and that is the concept of abundance. I don't think people understand the abundance concept because we can't understand how God integrated in his creation the ability to sustain and increase. I usually use nature to explain the concept of abundance. Did you know that an elephant eats 200 kg of vegetation a day? In the Kruger National Park there are 7000 elephants. That means they eat 1400 tons of vegetation per day—with plenty left for all the other animals. Can you believe that nature supply so much vegetation a day? About 70 trucks, fully loaded, just for what the elephants ate, not even counting all the other herbivores food needs. The trees and plants keep growing every day, and every day brings a fresh supply of food. Growth is an indication of being alive.

Like the forest, an economy also grows. For example, if you buy an item for R100 from somebody and sell it for R120 to somebody else, that means you make a profit of R20, and you have grown your money by R20. You can buy a property for R300 000 and sell it, after a period of time, for R380 000, and there is the magic again: your money has grown by R80 000. Let me explain this magic. Nature and money have several things in common. Plants grow, and so does an economy: the value of the property or asset that you bought will increase. Also, in nature trees will die, there will be droughts etc. In an economy, some properties lose their value or may not grow as much or as fast as expected. But over a period of time, there will be growth. And what personal effort do you have to make? Not much, except for maintaining the property; the benefit you get comes from the growth of the country's economy.

> **Proverbs 12:11** *Those who work their land will have abundant food, but those who chase fantasies have no sense.*

> **Proverbs 12:24** *Diligent hands will rule, but laziness ends in forced labour.*

When you work, you earn a salary; that means you receive money at the end of the month or week which you would not have had if you hadn't worked. When you are doing business by buying or selling products or by producing or manufacturing something, you get money by selling your product for more than it cost you. That means you are making a profit, which means you in fact create some extra money. That is the definition of productivity: you produce surpluses.

In this process of making money, you must give something back. Other people must benefit from your successes. God wants you to do this, you can't receive with a closed hand.

This is also in accordance with the concept of ubuntu, a Nguni word that was expanded into a philosophy in the eighties and nineties and is now often used in company boardrooms in Southern Africa. It means we are all interdependent, that "I am not fully me without you". To create involvement in the community you must make sure you are helping and giving guidance to others.

> *Matthew 6:2-5 So when you give to the needy, do not announce it with trumpets, as the hypocrites do in the synagogues and on the streets, to be honoured by others. Truly I tell you, they have received their reward in full. 3 But when you give to the needy, do not let your left hand know what your right hand is doing, so that your giving may be in secret. Then your Father, who sees what is done in secret, will reward you.*

You can share in this abundance. If your income is static, then it means your standard of living will be static. The only way to share in the Lord's abundance is to make an effort to grow, and that can be achieved when you are productive, doing business, creating employment. You have to grow your income when you work for a salary. Your priority expenses are normally very close to your earnings and leave little room for instalments to meet your credit obligations, but there are many ways of growing your salary. When you work hard and get promotion at work, or study hard and climb to higher positions in your company, you may over time achieve financial wellness. Everything takes time. If you plant a tree, it will only bear fruit after a certain period of time, and the same applies to farming with animals or manufacturing products.

When I visited Bangkok I was amazed to see how people with on bicycles transported huge loads of food or clothing to areas where they sold their goods. Some of them actually had regular jobs and ran their small businesses after working hours.

CHAPTER 4

THE NEGATIVE SPIRAL OF DEBT

A spiral is a line following path like a corkscrew. A negative spiral can be seen as a situation that gets worse and worse. It is very difficult to escape from such a situation; it is like a whirlpool that just pulls you in deeper and deeper.

When you look at Fig 1 you can see how it starts with falling into arrear; if you don't take action, you may become insolvent and you can only be rehabilitated after 5 years.

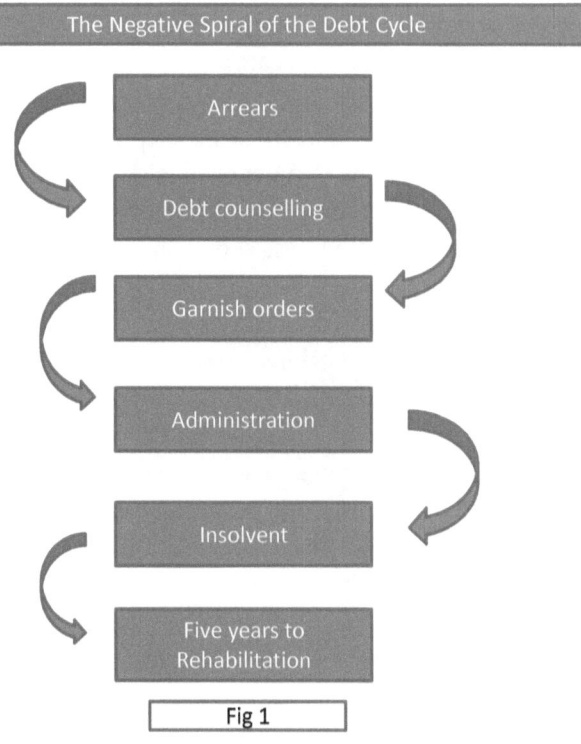

I have explained that credit can become your enemy, and that is exactly the impact it has if your debts become a burden which you can't carry any longer. Drastic steps are needed to get you out of this spiral. The current that pulls you further and further down is the continuous pressure from the creditors who insist on payment.

We regularly read in newspapers that people commit suicide or even murder their entire family because of financial difficulties, and in most cases it started with a credit transaction.

How do you deal with debt? Do you know how quickly you can end up in that whirlpool? Do you realise that debt can cause your financial death?

South Africans are known to take up credit very easily. And credit is very easy to get available in this country. Just look at all the adverts placed in the media by banks and other financial institutions, shops and all sorts of service providers. Everywhere you are invited to borrow money or apply for credit. The impression is created that money is there just for the taking. You can even get credit by telephone or e-mail.

Credit may be easy to get, but earning money is a different matter. You have to work very hard and very long, and with a strict savings plan, before you have earned a large amount of money that you can spend as you like. But this ability to spend at will does not continue forever; you will very soon discover that money tends to disappear very quickly.

In an interview, a very well-known soccer player who earns the incredible amount of just under R1 million a month said you wouldn't believe how quickly you would get into financial trouble the moment your income stream dried up. He said if you earned R10 000 a month, you would spend R10 000, and when you earned R600 000 a month you would spend that R600 000. That's what people do. We think it will last forever. Let's look at the following example.

If you earn R1000 a week, how many weeks must you work before you will be able to buy yourself a television and a bedroom suite of R15 000? Can we say 15 weeks? Certainly not, because you can't save your full salary every week and have R15 000 (R1 000 x 15 weeks) available after 15 weeks. You must first pay your living expenses. Let's assume your living expenses are R600; that means you can save R400 every week. That means that the time you need to have R15 000 available is 37, 5 weeks (9 months). During these nine months you must, of course, not spend money on anything else, not even on accidental events (sickness, unexpected expenses such as petrol or taxi fare increases etc.)

Saving up R15 000 will take you 9 months. You get the idea: real money is not easily available. It takes time and effort to earn.

On the other hand, getting a loan of R15 000 (capital amount) is easy if you earn a salary. It might take you only somewhere between one and three hours, and money will be transferred directly into your account.

But here's the sting in the tail: Now you have to pay that R15 000 back. You and the bank (or lending institution) signed an agreement about the payback terms, and these terms include the interest rate, credit life insurance (the financial institution will charge you a premium to insure your life, so that if you die your debt will be settled by the insurance company), an admin fee (they normally charge a fee for the processing of the transaction) and the payback period. If you want to repay the loan in the same 9 months as in our example above, you need to pay R475 per week. As we said, you can't afford that. So you come to an agreement with the bank to pay back R400 per week. But that means you will have to pay for about 7 weeks more, in other words a total of 44, 5 weeks. And the interest you pay to the bank amounts to R2586.00 (this amount does not include the credit life insurance and admin fee).

> **Numbers 30:2** *If a man vows a vow to the Lord, or swears an oath to bind himself by a pledge, he shall not break his word. He shall do according to all that proceeds out of his mouth.*

Here you can see the suction effect of the debt cycle:

- You pay 7 weeks longer on your debt!
- And for the privilege of having the money up front (or having the use of whatever you bought), you pay R2586,00 more than you borrowed.
- Keep in mind that if you pay credit life insurance and an admin fee, the payback can take longer and the amount that you have to pay back over and above your capital will be more too.

What will the effect be if the amount you borrowed increases to R150 000 or to R350 000? The period you are going to pay back is going to be much longer, and the interest you pay back will also be much more.

> *You have to understand the commitment you have to make and understand that you don't have money available for anything else.*

To understand this better you must understand the difference between *productive* interest and *passive* interest.

Like credit, interest is not a new concept. Students of ancient history have investigated early hunters and farmers to see what the payback was on the loans of cattle, seeds and tools in those days. This could indicate the amount of interest paid. They were not able to come up with a percentage for those days, but it was confirmed that interest was indeed paid. At first the practice of charging interest was based more on tribal customs than on formal economies, but in classical Greece and Rome (some 2 500 years ago) it was already an established practice.

Productive interest. Let's use a very simple example. If you buy a cow on credit, you will have to pay interest on the loan you made (the money you borrowed to buy the cow). Where will you get the money from to pay this interest? The cow produces milk, which you will be able use in the house, which means you don't need to buy milk any longer. Plus there might be enough milk for you to sell to someone who is in need of milk, which will create an income. The money a) saved by not buying milk and b) earned from milk you sell can be deducted from the interest you have to pay on the loan with which you bought the cow.

Passive interest. If you buy yourself a television set on credit, you will also have to pay interest on the loan. Where will the money come from to pay the interest? The television is not a productive asset—unlike with the cow, you can't make money with it, which means you have to take money from your salary or another source to pay this interest. Conclusion: buying an unproductive item will leave you with a shortfall which you need to fund from something else, like your salary or other products that you will have to sell. Your productive item will pay for itself, and you may even earn additional money from it.

Now let's look what happens if you don't pay your debt.

We can define debt as an amount of money that is still outstanding for an article you have already bought or for a service you have already received. As long as you pay your instalments in accordance with the agreement, there is no problem.

When you apply for a loan or credit, the lender (or future creditor) will very likely consult a credit bureau. A credit bureau collects credit information from certain sources and provides credit information about the public or organisations on demand. We have two credit bureaux in SA: TransUnion (formerly TransUnion ITC) and Experian.

The credit bureau's role is as follows:

o   If you apply for a loan, the credit provider will request a credit report to determine your creditworthiness.
o   If you don't pay your debt, the credit provider will forward your details to the bureau. That means you will be blacklisted.
o   If a credit application is approved, it will be uploaded on the ITC databases and will be updated every month.

Applying for credit must be a *calculated* risk. And it's you who must do the calculating. Always remember that the credit provider may not give you proper advice, because you are a potential customer and he will make huge profits out of you. The lender will not let you go; he will find a way to give you credit, because that's his business. Later in the book I will explain to you the importance of talking to the right people.

The problem starts when the client stops payment.

Let me explain the debt cycle[1]:

- You believe you need a specific article, but you can't afford to buy it cash.
- Let's assume you didn't do a proper personal budget and a needs analysis.
- You apply for credit and it is approved.
- After 3 months, you can't pay the instalment.
- You don't contact the credit supplier to inform him or to make special arrangements.
- The credit supplier can't get hold of you and reports you to a credit bureau. That means if you want to apply for credit from any other institution and they do a creditworthiness check, they will see that you owe money elsewhere and are not paying your instalments. The new application will not be approved.
- You now go to the first credit supplier, and perhaps they will agree to a new deal, which is called **consolidation of debt**. This sounds wonderful, because all your accounts are now placed in one account. Now you pay less per month, and although you will be paying over a longer period, the bottom line is that you can

---

[1]   I will put this into a flow chart as well.

survive again for another six months, depending on your commitment!

- You now realise you have money available every month, because you pay less on the outstanding debt. You decide to take up a new loan, and your new lender thinks you can afford it. He calculates the affordability of your new loan by deducting your living expenses and old and new instalments from your income, and if you still have money available for living expenses he will approve the loan.

- After six months the same thing happens. You can't pay your instalments and you avoid the credit supplier until you receive lots of final demands for payment.

- Consolidation is now impossible, but now you can go for debt counselling.

- You go and see a debt counsellor (this will be discussed in more detail in the next chapter). You are now, in a manner of speaking, in the **financial jail.** Depending on the sentence you are going to get, you will be financially dead. You will not be able to take part in the economy unless you do it in cash. The counsellor will suggest a few options, depending on your situation:

  o Rearrangement of debt; restructuring of debt; administration or
  o Insolvency.

What do these options mean?

Rearrangement of debt. You can, with or without the help of the debt counsellor, start discussions with the credit providers to structure an agreement to pay off your debt over a certain period. This can be done by law or by consent.

Restructuring of debt. This can only be done with the help of a debt counsellor and is a legal process. That means you will be legally bound to stick to the new payback agreement; if you default (skip a payment) you will expose yourself to a judgment or execution. The court allows you a period of up to 90 years to settle your debts. In effect, this means a sentence of 90 years in the **financial jail**. This can cost you up to R9000 plus a monthly fee, and you will be "financially dead" for the period the counsellor schedules your repayment.

Administration. An attorney will be appointed who will take all your accounts to the court and explain there that you can only afford a certain amount on instalments, which is normally very small. The judge will then place you under administration, which will mean the following:

- o A garnishee order will be made against your salary. This order sets an amount of money that will be deducted from your salary and paid over to the attorney to pay your creditors.
- o The attorney will be appointed as your administrator. He will collect the money deducted from your salary and pay it over to your creditors.
- o The attorney will collect a fee every month as his payment for the work. You will lose this money!

o   You will not be allowed to take up any credit unless the administrator gives you an approval letter. He may refuse to give you such a letter for the first two years, depending on your situation.

Insolvency. In this case all your assets—everything you own—are sold by auction. The proceeds from the auction are used to pay your creditors. If, for example, you owe one of your creditors R15 000, the curator may allocate only R9 000 to him as his share of the proceeds of the auction; the rest (R6 000) he must write off as bad debt. There will also be a court case, and the judge will declare your estate "sequestrated".

This means the following:

o   You will not be allowed credit for at least 5 years.
o   If you want to apply for any credit or financial activities, you need the approval of the curator (that is the person who sold all your assets and paid your creditors).
o   Going insolvent will cost you money, because the creditors may receive less than you owed them and that can mean it will take longer for you to be rehabilitated.
o   To get back into the financial world, you have to apply for rehabilitation. This also costs money. Nobody works for free—don't let anyone tell you different!

Now you can see what I mean when I say you are in **financial jail**. You will go to work and you will come home as in the past, but neither you nor your wife will have any say about how your money is spent. You will have no financial freedom and you will be forced into a commitment by somebody else. Your financial freedom is taken away by somebody else, and only that somebody else can give it back to you—when he feels you have met the objective set by him.

Wouldn't you rather be the one who decides your own destiny? You *can* set your own objectives! You can make the same type of commitment, but with the difference that it's you and your family who make the decisions without getting into **financial jail**.

If you want to get out of the debt cycle, read on!

CHAPTER 5

HOW TO MANAGE YOUR SPENDING

Psalm 37:5 *Commit your way to the Lord; trust in him, and he will act.*

An organisation by the name of Octogen did research in South Africa and came to the following conclusion on how people are currently spending their money. You can use this as a guideline for spending your money, although I will discuss other methods as well.

SUGGESTED SPENDING

Debt payments (house, vehicle and other accounts)		**35%**
Insurance, medical fund & unit trust		**25%**
Household expenses, e.g.		**35%**
Groceries*	8%	

Water & lights	3%	
Travel	6%	
Telephone	3%	
Entertainment	4%	
Rates	2%	
School fees	6%	
Domestic worker	2%	
Security	1%	
Emergency fund		**5%**

*These expenses add up to 35%, but they are estimates and can differ from household to household. In principle, you should stay within the 35% bracket.

Now you have a broad idea of how your spending must fit into a suggested framework. Let us take an example:

We assume your net salary is R12 000 and that no credit instalments are deducted.

Type of expense	Net pay	% used	Budget
Debt payments	R12 000	35%	R4200
Insurance etc.	R12 000	35%	R4200
Household expenses	R12 000	20%	R2400
Emergency fund	R12 000	5%	R 600

Keep in mind that this is just a guideline. You may choose to cut back on one item in order to spend more on something else, but you may not go beyond of certain limits. People will often cancel their insurance, which is an enormous risk; the assets that you worked so hard to pay off for many years could be lost in seconds. If you don't budget to cover them, they will be lost and you will be set back a couple of years, which in turn will not allow you to grow. Recovering takes time and money!

Your basic needs are determined by your household expenses and insurance premiums. Normally you can't really avoid any of these costs, but you can nevertheless evaluate and decide if there are any you can cut or go without. When you budget, it is best to take the previous year's expenditure and use that to forecast the expenditure of the following year.

> **Proverbs 16:3** *Commit your work to the Lord,*
> *and your plans will be established.*

Another method people use to manage their expenditure is using envelopes. The envelope is used as a sort of savings account, which has a balance and will only be used for a specific expense; when the money is finished, there is no money available for that specific expense. I know many families who use envelopes to manage their finances. They have an envelope for each expense. Each envelope is marked "school fees", "milk", "bread", "telephone", "transport", "chocolates" etc. The amount they decided to spend on that specific item is then put into the envelope. If the money in the envelope is spent before payday, they just don't buy those articles until the next month, when money will be put into the envelope again. If the money for bread is finished, they can go without bread, but if the money for transport is finished, that is a serious problem, because the parents need to go to work.

The biggest advantage of the envelope method is that you can see exactly where the money is spent and what is available after each spend. When you use a debit or credit card, you don't see the spending unless you keep a proper record for each and every transaction. Remember, in the case of card there is always an admin fee with each and every transaction, and there may be finance costs as well.

That means that at the beginning of the month, it is important to prioritise the expenses properly and not to use the money set aside for the high-priority expenses (transport) for a low-priority expense (chocolates). What so often happens is that money is spent on low—priority items in the first week or two of the month, and then the money set aside for transport is put at risk. If the finances are not properly planned and managed, you may be forced to borrow money somewhere to at least get you to work. If you call for help from Mr Credit, you must be aware that he will put pressure on your finances in future. The moment you start with credit, you have taken the first step into the debt spiral, and you can only stay out of this whirlpool with very intelligent planning.

So often people run to the casino during these difficult times, taking their last few bucks to try their luck on the gambling machines. Most of the time they have to go home with no money at all. Thomas J. Stanley, in his book "The Millionaire Mind", stated that after speaking to thousands of millionaires worldwide, he had not found even one who had made his fortune by gambling. What are the chances that you are going to make it? They say the chance of dying is greater than the chance of winning the lotto . . .

Becoming addicted to gambling can be just as bad as drugs or alcohol abuse. Casinos were invented not to make you rich, but the owners, and the gold membership card, free drinks and accommodation, free credit if you join etc. are just ways of getting you hooked. Everything in life starts small; a little bet here, another little bet there—and you will keep feeding the monster until it kills you. Quite recently a well-known friend of mine lost his work and all his possessions because of gambling, and I am sure he may well lose his family too.

It may be a good idea to start the "envelop strategy" in your household. Even if you only do it for six months, so that you can exactly see what you spend your money on. After you have gathered this info, you can work on a final budget. Then you can transfer or withdraw the money as when needed from your bank account or pay it with your credit card because you have the discipline. Just remember, you must keep a record of each and every transaction that you do and make provision for the bank charges. Keep the withdrawal or transfer slip that you get from the bank or ATM and record your transactions from those slips.

There is a saying—and is has been tested—that if you want to change a habit, you must give it up for 40 days, and you will never do it again. Therefore, if you want to acquire a new habit you must make sure you practise it consistently for 40 days, and it will be part of your life.

Buy only what you need!

You can afford only what you can get with the money left after you have covered your basic needs (priority expenses). The more you have left after paying for your basic needs, the better your position will be: you will have surplus income, some money left after your priority expenses have been paid.

People often buy a car or house that is too expensive or a plasma television instead of an ordinary television. Be careful not to spend money on stuff you don't need or can't afford in the long term.

Everybody has a dream; if you don't have one, get yourself one, because that is your drive in life. I always remember the last part of the beautiful film "Pretty Woman", where the tall gentleman walks across the street and the end of the movie says: "Keep on dreaming. Some dreams come true and some don't, but keep on dreaming." Did you ever listen to the song "Impossible Dream" by Phil Collins? Everything is possible: if you can think it, you can achieve it. This dream might be a beautiful house or an expensive car. whatever it is, it becomes your objective or goal; work towards it. It becomes easier if you break it up into achievable bits and celebrate the small wins. You will get to that goal.

When we start working on a recovery plan or budget, I need you to think positively. Part of being qualified to manage your spending is your brain power, the way you think.

You have to have faith in yourself and your family that you will be able to pull this through. Faith is the basis you are going to stand on, and your thinking will be the fuel taking you forward.

Let us define faith. Whether you are a Christian or not, most people believe in some sort of creator of the universe and believe that this creator cares for them and has certain special powers we human beings don't have. I am going to explain it from the perspective of a Christian.

Faith is defined in Hebrews 11 verse 1: "Now faith is confidence in what we hope for and assurance about what we do not see". That may be one of the main reasons why humans struggle with faith; we prefer to say: "seeing is believing and touching is reality". How wrong we are, when the Lord points out to us that we have to believe without seeing. Just practise this in your life. You have to deliberately make sure that you stand steadfast in your beliefs.

Robert H. Schuller, in his book "Tough Minded Faith for Tender Hearted People" explains faith so appropriately. We all want proof of God's existence and abilities—but when we have proof, there is no longer room for belief, for faith believes in that which cannot be proven. He sums it up in one sentence "When proof is possible, faith becomes impossible".

I am going to give you the recipe to get rich out of this debt spiral you are caught in, but I need your unconditional faith in whatever the final plan is going to be to make it come true. When you develop your plan and you do it in faith and you set yourself reasonably achievable targets, you will win.

> **Luke 9:62** *Jesus said to him, "No one who puts his hand to the plough and looks back is fit for the kingdom of God."*

We now need one more ingredient, and that is your thinking. Your thinking will be confronted with that little voice inside you which we call "self-talk". I believe you have already heard it. Surely, when you started reading this book it must have confronted you with thoughts such as: "Who is this guy writing this book who wants to tell me I must do this or that?" or: "No man, this is not possible!" and so on. What are you thinking now? Stop reading for a moment and listen to that voice. Is it positive or negative? Just remember, you are in control of that voice. Simply change your thinking!

Let me explain. I would like to compare your thinking to a radio station. You tune your radio to a certain frequency and get a music broadcast. If you don't like the music you just change the frequency, and there you are—tuned to a totally different station, perhaps a talk show. Just check your thinking; if you are thinking thoughts that make you feel miserable, get another station.

Many people use affirmations to get themselves out of those negative thinking patterns. An affimation can be five or ten sentences or words that you repeat every morning, like:

- There is an abundance of money in the world.
- The more money I make, the more money everyone makes.
- God wants me to be rich.

- I create wealth in a spiritual way.
- The more money I make, the more money I give.
- I am blessed with an abundance of joy and happiness.
- I believe.

Challenge that little voice with these affirmations, and you will see how quickly it disappears. You can't win a race by telling yourself "I am going to lose this race" all the time; you have to be positive.

We are going to need money and time to get you out of the debt spiral, and that requires patience. It is absolutely important that you stay in control of your own destination. When your financial situation is already in the legal eagles' hands, they are going to set the pace, because you are already in financial jail; and that means they decide for you, as they believe you are unable to decide on your own. If you are still in control, then maybe we will get you out quicker, but it still going to be a tough time, and that is why you must make sure your mind (thinking) is tuned into the correct station.

CHAPTER 6

HOW TO BUDGET

> **Luke 14:28-30** *"For which of you, intending to build a tower, does not sit down first and count the cost, whether he has enough to finish it—lest, after he has laid the foundation, and is not able to finish, all who see it begin to mock him, saying 'This man began to build and was not able to finish'?"*

We already did a form of budgeting when we discussed the household expenses, and you may already have a very good idea of how we going to draft the budget. A budget is a plan; you will have to sit down and take time to consider how you are going to spend your money in future.

A budget consists of three mayor quantities: the budget figure, the actual figure and the variance. I will take one expense item (electricity) and explain the three concepts with amounts.

- We **budget** for electricity costs of R1 000,00 per month.
- If the **actual** expense is R1 000,00 per month, then the. **variance** is zero (R0,00).
- If the **actual** expense is R1 600,00 per month, then the **variance** will be a **shortfall** of R600 (R 1000,00 minus R1 600.00). That means you spent more than you budgeted for and you will have to find a way to get that extra money.
- If the **actual** expense is R800,00 per month, then the **variance** will be a **surplus** of R200 (R1 000,00 minus R800,00). That means you have R200 available on your income to pay other expenses.

It is clear from this example that if you budget incorrectly for electricity, you might have a shortfall every month, and you will have to find an additional R600 every month.

> **Proverbs 13:16** *A wise man thinks ahead; a fool doesn't, and even brags about it!*

Budgets are mainly about figures, amounts you must find and slot into your plan, But there are a lot of other "softer" issues behind the budget which I need to share with you; in fact this is more important. You need to understand that budgeting is your roadmap to financial wellness. You must be committed to the following:

- draft the budget as accurately as humanly possible;
- then pay your expenses exactly according to the plan;
- determine the variances every month;

- find ways and means to reduce the negative variances, and
- do this EVERY MONTH.

This is like a gym program or a diet: you have to stick to the plan regrettably; people don't do it unless it has become a lifestyle.

There are three very important aspects that you need to make provision for in your budget, namely:

1. Pay yourself first (which I will discuss in the next chapter).
2. You have to save money.
3. You have to give to the poor.

I have already referred to the above in the opening chapters of this book.

Savings

South Africa is a country with one of the world's lowest savings rates; we currently spend 76% of our household income on debt. You must understand that debt is very expensive; you must pay all the additional costs, such as interest, credit life insurance premiums, admin fees etc.

On the other hand, when you start saving money you will earn interest, and once you get into the habit you will create a huge reserve from which you will able to finance from your own pocket whatever you need. No more financing or credit costs!

> *Genesis 41:34-36* Let Pharaoh appoint
> commissioners over the land to take a fifth of
> the harvest of Egypt during the seven years of
> abundance. They should collect all the food of
> these good years that are coming and store up
> the grain under the authority of Pharaoh, to
> be kept in the cities for food. This food should
> be held in reserve for the country, to be used
> during the seven years of famine that will
> come upon Egypt, so that the country may not
> be ruined by the famine.

> *Proverbs 21:20* The wise store up choice food
> and olive oil, but fools gulp theirs down.

You must give to the poor.

Jesus said the poor will always be with us. We need to understand and help them.

I have read any number of books on personal finance; money etc., and I have not come across a single one that does not refer to the responsibility we have to give. It cuts across religions and cultures: you have to give in order to receive. There are any number of examples and stories of how people benefited after they started giving with an open heart—and 'open heart' means to expect nothing in return. I need to share with you a few sayings from the Bible about this point.

> *2 Corinthians 9:7* Each man should give what he
> has decided in his heart to give, not reluctantly or
> under compulsion, for God loves a cheerful giver.

Luke 6:32-35 *"If you love those who love you, what credit is that to you? Even 'sinners' love those who love them. And if you do good to those who are good to you, what credit is that to you? Even 'sinners' do that. And if you lend to those from whom you expect repayment, what credit is that to you? Even 'sinners' lend to 'sinners,' expecting to be repaid in full. But love your enemies, do good to them, and lend to them without expecting to get anything back. Then your reward will be great, and you will be sons of the Most High, because he is kind to the ungrateful and wicked.*

Back to the budget.

Drawing up a budget is quite easy.

> Step 1: Write down the rand value of all your income and get the total.
> Step 2: Write down all your expenses and the total.
> Step 3: Deduct the expenses from the income. A positive amount will mean you have a surplus and a negative means you have a shortfall.

All three steps are in the example in Table 1. The table is self-explanatory. If you read the Action Column and the Identifier Column, it will explain the calculations in the table. Your type of expense will differ from the example, but try to define it in the same way we did in the example split your expenses in fixed expenses and variable expenses. The Fixed expenses are those expenses that will not change every month like your Rent for your house while Variable expenses will be changing every month like your electricity because every month you will have different usage.

Normally you can save on your variable costs, but not on your fixed cost. Your rent you pay every month is fixed, but your electricity cost depends on your usage, therefore it is variable—and you can manage (control) it.

Table 1

The budget for Mr				
Detail	Action	R value	R value	Identifier
Gross salary			**15 000.00**	A
Less deductions (excluding any instalments on your household			3 500.00	B
Net salary	A-B		**11 500.00**	C
Plus additional Income	E+F		—	D
additional Income 1			—	E
additional Income 2			—	F
Total Income	C+F		**11 500.00**	G
Less total expenses	I+J		**9 620.00**	H
Fixed expenses		5 300.00		I
Your contribution for yourself		500.00		
Your contribution for outside		500.00		
Rent/installment house		3 500.00		
Emergency fund		250.00		
Vehicle installment		—		
Short term insurance premium		—		
Insurance life/funeral scheme		250.00		

DSTV/Mnet		300.00		
Rates and taxes		—		
School fees		—		
Variable expenses		4 320.00		J
Groceries		2 200.00		
Electricity		500.00		
Transport cost (taxi fare/fuel)		1 200.00		
Telephone (cell and landline)		300.00		
Entertainment		120.00		
Surplus or Shortage	G-H		**1 880.00**	K

When you deduct the expenses from the income, you will have either a surplus or a shortage.

Surplus: Decide how this money will be spent. The best way will be to add it to your savings account and not waste it on unnecessary items. In this example we already made provision for "paying yourself" and making a contribution to outside people like the church or people in need. That means Mr A still has R1 880,00 available. If he has the discipline to stay within his budget for six months, he will have saved R11 280. See table 2.

Shortage: Most people end up with a shortage. There are two major reasons for this:

- Your income is too low and has to be increased. Increasing your income if you only depend on your salary is very difficult; you work for a fixed salary and you only receive annual increases and (in some cases) an annual bonus; or you are spending too much and you need to decrease your expenditure. Most of the time, you have 100% control over your expenses, except for unforeseen disasters such as accidents or the like. But there are ways and means to manage those as well; if you can commit a certain amount and some time to that emergency, you will also overcome it.

Since you can control your expenses, it is clear that we need to do some analysis on them. I mentioned elsewhere that there are certain principles that must be followed to get out of the negative (downward) debt spiral. Of course proper budgeting will help, but this is not enough. We will have to consider each action we take thoroughly when we draw up the budget, because you have to make that action part of your life; it must become a way of living. Budgeting cannot be a mere theoretical exercise; it needs to become part of your daily activities, and your family must be part of it.

Many people make the mistake of writing down all the expenses they have to pay at the end of the month instead of planning the monthly expenses for a whole year ahead. You should not incur any expense unless you have planned for it; in principle, if the expense is not approved, you may not incur it. The approval of the expense falls within your authority, unlike in a company, where two or three persons must approve any budgeted expenditure. If the expense was not budgeted for, even more people might be required to approve it. You need to be very strict in your personal life about buying things which were not budgeted for. I often repeat this in this book: you can't spend money you don't have. I recently spoke to a friend of mine whose daughter completed her degree year a couple of years ago.

Now, at age 25, she has bought herself a house of over R1 million, and the only principle she applied was that of saving money. When she bought her first car, she paid double the instalment every month and had paid it off in 24 months. She then saved the amount of the remaining instalments in her dad's house bond. Those savings she used as a deposit on her house. As a youngster, you want to do so many things—you want to buy yourself jewellery, an expensive cellphone, an IPad etc. Just look what young adults spend their money on: in most instances on once-off gratification and not on something that increases their net asset value (the difference between your total assets and what you still have to pay).

If you can't afford something, please don't buy it, and if you didn't plan to buy something, please don't.

During the next few pages I am going to teach you a lifestyle. Depending how well you understand the implications of the "financial jail", the more you will be ready to make these changes in your life.

Table 2

The budget for Mr.____	January			February			March			April			May			June		
Detail	Budget	Actual	Deviation	Budget	Actual	Deviation	Budget	Actual	Deviation	Budget	Actual	Deviation	Budget	Actual	Deviation	Budget	Actual	Deviation
Gross salary	15 000.00	15 000.00	-	15 000.00	15 000.00	-	15 000.00	15 000.00	-	15 000.00	15 000.00	-	15 000.00	15 000.00	-	15 000.00	15 000.00	-
Less deductions (excluding any instalments on your household)	3 500.00	3 500.00	-	3 500.00	3 500.00	-	3 500.00	3 500.00	-	3 500.00	3 500.00	-	3 500.00	3 500.00	-	3 500.00	3 500.00	-
Net salary	11 500.00	11 500.00	-	11 500.00	11 500.00	-	11 500.00	11 500.00	-	11 500.00	11 500.00	-	11 500.00	11 500.00	-	11 500.00	11 500.00	-
Plus additional Income	-	-	-	-	-	-	-	-	-	-	-	-	-	-	-	-	-	-
additional Income 1	-	-	-	-	-	-	-	-	-	-	-	-	-	-	-	-	-	-
additional Income 2	-	-	-	-	-	-	-	-	-	-	-	-	-	-	-	-	-	-
Total Income	11 500.00	11 500.00	-	11 500.00	11 500.00	-	11 500.00	11 500.00	-	11 500.00	11 500.00	-	11 500.00	11 500.00	-	11 500.00	11 500.00	-
Less total expenses	9 620.00	9 620.00	-	9 620.00	9 620.00	-	9 620.00	9 620.00	-	9 620.00	9 620.00	-	9 620.00	9 620.00	-	9 620.00	9 620.00	-
Fixed expenses	5 300.00	5 300.00	-	5 300.00	5 300.00	-	5 300.00	5 300.00	-	5 300.00	5 300.00	-	5 300.00	5 300.00	-	5 300.00	5 300.00	-
Your contribution for yourself	500.00	500.00	-	500.00	500.00	-	500.00	500.00	-	500.00	500.00	-	500.00	500.00	-	500.00	500.00	-
Your contribution for outside	500.00	500.00	-	500.00	500.00	-	500.00	500.00	-	500.00	500.00	-	500.00	500.00	-	500.00	500.00	-
Rent/installment house	3 500.00	3 500.00	-	3 500.00	3 500.00	-	3 500.00	3 500.00	-	3 500.00	3 500.00	-	3 500.00	3 500.00	-	3 500.00	3 500.00	-
Emergency fund	250.00	250.00	-	250.00	250.00	-	250.00	250.00	-	250.00	250.00	-	250.00	250.00	-	250.00	250.00	-
Vehicle installment	-	-	-	-	-	-	-	-	-	-	-	-	-	-	-	-	-	-
Short term insurance premium	-	-	-	-	-	-	-	-	-	-	-	-	-	-	-	-	-	-
Insurance life/funeral scheme	250.00	250.00	-	250.00	250.00	-	250.00	250.00	-	250.00	250.00	-	250.00	250.00	-	250.00	250.00	-
DSTV/Mnet	300.00	300.00	-	300.00	300.00	-	300.00	300.00	-	300.00	300.00	-	300.00	300.00	-	300.00	300.00	-
Rates and taxes	-	-	-	-	-	-	-	-	-	-	-	-	-	-	-	-	-	-
School fees	-	-	-	-	-	-	-	-	-	-	-	-	-	-	-	-	-	-
Variable expenses	4 320.00	4 320.00	-	4 320.00	4 320.00	-	4 320.00	4 320.00	-	4 320.00	4 320.00	-	4 320.00	4 320.00	-	4 320.00	4 320.00	-
Groceries	2 200.00	2 200.00	-	2 200.00	2 200.00	-	2 200.00	2 200.00	-	2 200.00	2 200.00	-	2 200.00	2 200.00	-	2 200.00	2 200.00	-
Electricity	500.00	500.00	-	500.00	500.00	-	500.00	500.00	-	500.00	500.00	-	500.00	500.00	-	500.00	500.00	-
Transport cost (taxi fare/fuel)	1 200.00	1 200.00	-	1 200.00	1 200.00	-	1 200.00	1 200.00	-	1 200.00	1 200.00	-	1 200.00	1 200.00	-	1 200.00	1 200.00	-
Telephone (cell and landline)	300.00	300.00	-	300.00	300.00	-	300.00	300.00	-	300.00	300.00	-	300.00	300.00	-	300.00	300.00	-
Entertainment	120.00	120.00	-	120.00	120.00	-	120.00	120.00	-	120.00	120.00	-	120.00	120.00	-	120.00	120.00	-
Surplus or Shortage	1 880.00	1 880.00	-	1 880.00	1 880.00	-	1 880.00	1 880.00	-	1 880.00	1 880.00	-	1 880.00	1 880.00	-	1 880.00	1 880.00	-

Cash Flow	Jan		Febr		March		April		May		June	
Starting Balance	-		1 880.00		3 760.00		5 640.00		7 520.00		9 400.00	
Inflow/outflow	1 880.00		1 880.00		1 880.00		1 880.00		1 880.00		1 880.00	
Ending Balance	1 880.00		3 760.00		5 640.00		7 520.00		9 400.00		11 280.00	

Explanation of Table 2

	January	
Budget	Actual	Variance

For every month you will have to complete three columns.

Budget column:
- You determine the amount that you expect to receive (in the case of income) or to pay out (in the case of an expense) and enter it in the budget column.

Actual column:
- At the end of the month you record the actual amount you received or spent on the item for that specific month.

Variance:
- Here you want to determine the difference between the amount you budgeted and what really (actually) happened.
- In the case of income, you subtract the budget amount from the actual amount. For example you budget for R1000 in income and you receive R1100. That means the actual income (R1100) less the budget income (R1000) = R100 more than you budgeted. This means you are R100 better off.
- In the case of an expense, you subtract the actual amount from the budgeted amount. For example, you budgeted R300 for electricity but you paid R450. That means your budget expense (R300)

less your actual expense (R450) = minus R150, which means you spent R150 more than you budgeted, and you are R150 short.

- The variance column will indicate to you which area is the problem area and where you must be more cautious not to overspend.

Explanation of items reflected in the budget (Table 2).

The budget for Mr	
Detail	
Gross salary	This is the basic salary plus overtime and other allowance paid to you
Less deductions (Excluding any instalments on your household	You may have certain deduction from your salary that has nothing to do with your employment but you made arrangement that this amount may be deducted from your salary. This is in fact relate directly to your household expense and should seperately be indicated in your budget.
Net Salary	This is your Net take home pay, normally this amount will deposited in your bank account
Plus Additional Income	When you generate some additional income like "private work" or business you fill it in here. It is discussed in detail in the book.
Additional Income 1	Indicate your income seperately
Additional Income 2	Indicate your income seperately
Total Income	All income added together
Less Total Expenses	All expenses added together
Fixed Expenses	These are expenses that will not change for at least a year or longer
Your contribution for yourself	Explained in the book
Your contribution for outside	Explained in the book
Rent/Installment house	Self explanatory
Emergency fund	Explained in the book
Vehicle intallment	Self explanatory
Insurance short term	This a premium you pay to cover your moveable assets against theft, fire, accidents or natural disaster
Insurance life / Funeral scheme	This cover on your life and funerals in your family
DSTV / Mnet	Self explanatory
Rates and Taxes	If you own a house you must pay thess costs to local government
School fees	Self explanatory
Variable expenses	These are expenses that will change on a month to month basis and you will have some control over it.
Groceries	Self explanatory
Elektricity	Self explanatory
Transport cost (Taxi fare/Fuel)	Self explanatory
Telephone (Cell and Landline)	Self explanatory
Entertainment	Be careful here stay in your budget we spen to easily money on this (sigarettes, parties, alcohol etc). We hide these cost often with our groceries
Surplus or Shortage	With a surplus we have extra money available, and with a shortage we need money to pay all our expenses
Cash Flow	As the money flow in and out of your household it leave a positive or negative result. This example is positive because you can see how the money get more image it was negative then you could see what amount would be needed over a short period of time.
Starting Balance	In this example it indicate that the person has no money in the bank account. You can just reflect the amount that you have available
Inflow/outflow	This indicate if you have a surplus the end of the month which is then a inflow and if it was a shortage it would be an outflow
Ending Balance	This is the starting balance and inflow added together (it can also be a subtract calculation depending if it is a negative balance or an outflow). This ending balance will be your starting balance for the next month.

The difficult part of compiling a budget is to do the estimates and calculations. After that you must have the ability to assess and manage your budget.

Estimates

You have to plan for the rest of the year. You have to determine what will happen in each and every month. Sit with the family, find out what is needed in every month and decide if you are going to allow the expense or not; if you allow it, write it under your expenses and in the month in which it will be incurred.

> **Philippians 4:19** *And my God will supply every need of yours according to his riches in glory in Christ Jesus.*

If you keep proper records of this year, it will be much easier to do the planning for the next year, because you will have historical information available. Remember, the more accurately you predict, the better you will manage your finances. You are creating your own destination!

Be careful and honest with yourself; don't hide away expenses. We sometimes buy sweets for the children, but call them groceries, or we buy clothes or beer on the groceries expense. Groceries should be a necessity, not entertainment or luxury goods. I understand the principle: you walk into these big chain stores such as Pick 'n Pay and you buy everything under one roof. That's fine; the products might be cheaper here than in the smaller shops. When you come home, take the cash invoice (till slip), on which all the products are listed, and list the items and the relevant amounts under the different expenses (be specific) as set in your budget. Then you will see where the deviations are. Let me just underline this again: I don't say stop smoking (which would be a healthy thing to do); I am just saying: budget for it. If you know you are going to spend money on something, don't hide it away; indicate it on your budget, then there will be no surprises.

CHAPTER 7

THE FINANCIAL
WELLNESS RECOVERY PLAN

Colossians 3:17 *And whatever you do, in word or deed, do everything in the name of the Lord Jesus, giving thanks to God the Father through him.*

This could also be called your future financial wellness plan; it depends on what your current situation is. If you are already in the debt spiral, then it will be a financial wellness recovery plan, because I have to get you out of that spiral. If you are not in a financial crisis yet, then we will call it a future financial wellness plan.

Whichever plan you are going to work on, you must remember one very important principle:

> *YOU MUST STAY **PERSONALLY** IN CONTROL OF YOUR FINANCIAL MANAGEMENT.*

I see so many adverts along the highways, in magazines and in newspapers, which promise that if you visit their offices, they will make you rich and they will see that all your debts get paid. Please realise that it is only you who going to pay your debts. They will take control of your finances and will simply determine what amount you must pay to whom and over which term. Well, you can do this yourself, can't you? And remember, they don't work for free. You are going to pay them a fee or commission; therefore it will take you even longer to pay back your debts. The South African government is currently (August 2013) planning to give debtors amnesty whereby all recorded debt will deleted from the credit bureaux's lists, clearing the way for them to borrow money again. It all sounds great—but if these people have not learnt the principles of financial management, they will not benefit from the amnesty at all. That was proven when the government did the same a couple of years ago: within a very short period of time about 80% of those people were listed again.

How to stay in control of your financial management

There are a few rules which you must always follow if you want to stay in control:

- Pay yourself first.
- Talk to people who have financial and business knowledge.
- Buy what you can afford.
- Only buy what is needed (distinguish between a need and desire (greed or avarice).
- Always pay your creditors.

- Look after the needy.
- Agree with your family to make commitments.

Pay yourself first

This rule has two aspects we have to pay attention to: investing in yourself and looking after your family well and responsibly. Paying yourself does not mean treating or spoiling yourself—buying yourself a chocolate, having your hair or your nails done. These are just short-term benefits. Investing in yourself refers to saving money in your own name in a savings account, unit trust etc. Money you save or invest will return money to you in future; those other treats will have only temporary value. A car is a depreciating asset, while a house will increase in value. Go read "Rich Dad Poor Dad" by Robert T. Kiyosaki. Make sure you invest your money in such a manner that it will always pay you back.

> **Leviticus 27:32** *And every tithe of herds and flocks, every tenth animal of all that pass under the herdsman's staff, shall be holy to the Lord.*

Talk to people who have the knowledge

Investing money is not child's play. Make sure you talk to the right people. Where do you go for advice? Normally this would be a person you can trust. In the old days, people went to the local preacher or teacher for advice; these people were better educated, older and had wider experience than most others. Today there are many people around us with vast experience who are just as capable to advise us.

Unfortunately, there are also people who think they know everything about a topic or are blatantly cheating you.

I had that experience myself. I decided to buy an estate agency franchise, and the franchisor promised full support to make sure that his brand would become well known—one of my concerns was that his brand was not established country wide. When I studied the contracts, I was sure that he would give proper advice and would be actively involved in developing the brand. He promised that he would help with certain marketing campaigns in our area which he believed would help establish the brand. I believed in him so much that I decided to buy two areas, which meant I doubled my exposure. After about two months I realised that he had been lying; he did not want to help with any marketing campaign. I contacted my attorney, and his first question was: why didn't I come and ask him before I signed the contract? Needless to say, the franchisor stuck to the letter of the contract and all the promises made were empty words.

Then I contacted FASA (the Franchise Association of South Africa), but because the franchisor wasn't a member of FASA they couldn't help me. There I was, totally stranded. I had to close down the franchises and took a loss of R500 000. What had I done wrong? First of all, I should have given the contracts to my lawyer, contacted FASA right from the beginning and asked them about the risks when opening a franchise.

Before you do anything, get advice from the right people. Check their qualifications, get their track record and ask for references or referrals. Check if there is a watchdog organisation that oversees certain businesses or professions. In the insurance industry, you will find the Insurance and FAIS (Financial Advisory and Intermediary Services Act) ombudsman. In the finance sector, you will find the FSB (Financial Services Board) and in the estate agency industry you will find the IEASA (Institute for Estate Agents in South Africa). You can take your queries to these organisations to help with advice. There are many organisations that specifically look after the protection of the consumer. Find these institutions and report your problem to or discuss it with them.

In the case of debt, there are debt counsellors who are registered with the NCR (National Credit Regulator). The NCR also looks after the interests of the general public. You can visit their web page at the address www.ncr.org. za, for their contact details. They also provide information on your rights and give consumer tips, and you will be able to lodge a complaint by sending them an email at complaints@ncr.org.za

Buy what you can afford

The most common reason for rejecting a loan application is affordability. People buy because they want something, not because they need it. You need to distinguish between 'must have' and 'nice to have'. We all know children do not understand this difference, and time and again I see how the little ones manipulate the parents to buy what they want and not what they need. Unfortunately very few parents stop this behaviour.

Take note of the following examples. If you ask a man whether he really needs to buy that car, he will answer "I must have it". When you ask a lady whether she really needs to buy another pair of shoes, she will answer "I must have it"! You need to be objective and make sure you spend your money on what is needed. Remember, 'must have' means I can't carry on without it. Use this as a criterion. When you are in a shop and see something you would like to buy, don't buy it immediately; come back the next day—if you still need it, buy it then!

A survey was done on impulse buying a few years go. When a customer was leaving a shop with his trolley or shopping bags, they asked the shopper what products he had come to buy. They found that most people had bought more that they had intended to buy. In the case of women, their impulse buying was as low as 47%, while for men it was as high as 87%. Men can be the culprits; so men, control yourselves!

The budget you compile is a plan setting out how you will spend your money during the next month, six months or year.

The budget must lead you in your decision-making process. Stay within your boundaries; we can easily make a decision on the spur of the moment, only to realise later on we could have spent our money more wisely.

> **Proverbs 3:9-10** *Honour the Lord with your wealth and with the first fruits of all your produce; then your barns will be filled with plenty, and your vats will be bursting with wine.*

Only buy what is needed

Distinguish between need and desire. A need is what you can't go without. It is easy to persuade oneself that what one desires is something we can't go without; there are many examples of this in this book. The terms 'greed' and 'avarice' define desire very clearly. Don't be greedy! More is not always best.

Always pay you creditors

I have already said a lot about this. Remember, in ancient times you could become a slave if you did not pay your creditor. This has not changed much; when you are in financial jail, your financial freedom is curtailed. Somebody else will dictate your spending patterns.

Look after the needy

> **James 1:27** *Religion that is pure and undefiled before God, the Father, is this: to visit orphans and widows in their affliction, and to keep oneself unstained from the world.*

One of the rules you find in the Scriptures is that you must give your tithes and that God loves people with a giving spirit. What does that mean?

Look around you. You will always see people who are worse off than you, and there will always be those who are better off than you. People need help, and there must be a way you can help them. Victor Frankl, one of the greatest philosophers of our times, who was interned in a Nazi concentration camp, said that as long as one can mean and/or do something for other people, one will be able to survive. To live a meaningful life, you must mean something to somebody else. Focus on that; give and you will be amazed how blessed you will be.

Agree with your family to make commitments

The amounts you pay out every month can be too large, which means you must cut back on your expenses, and that implies you have to lower your lifestyle. The moment I say this, most people don't want to listen to me any longer. Yet it is interesting how easily you can find ways the family can save when you evaluate the family's lifestyle. You must be critical. The husband should not blame his wife or vice versa; everybody must accept responsibility. I remember how, when South Africa experienced the electricity crisis in January 2008, people complained there was no way they could save electricity. Surprisingly, after a couple of months tips on saving electricity popped up regularly on radio stations, television, in newspapers etc. If you have to survive, you will find a way to cut back on expenses, in other words, to save.

Do your problems lie with the fixed or variable costs? If the fixed costs are too high, then you have definitely made a commitment to something you can't afford—an expensive house, motor vehicle etc. You have to get out of that deal, and the sooner the better. If you had initially drawn up a proper budget, you would have known you could not afford it.

When your variable costs are too high, it might be necessary to cut back on your living expenses. The question here is: What can I afford? It is very important not to overspend. Lower your standard of living or increase your income.

You need to cut back on living expenses as a family. That is the only way you will be able to carry out your recovery plan.

How possible is this? Why must I do it? I will never be able to cut back! These are all questions that will run through your mind, but you will be able to answer them all if you focus on finding solutions and fully commit yourself. There's an old saying: everything the mind can conceive, it can achieve.

When I was still a youngster, there were no computers in the business world. We were only allowed to use a calculator in our third year in Financial Accounting after we had a huge argument with Professor Els. In those days, it was said that you couldn't take three weeks' leave because when you came back to work, your post would have been abolished because the computer had taken over that job. If I told you how many people we know were retrenched in those years because of that, you'd call me a liar. I know of a person who started selling vegetables, and we all thought he was never going to make it. I mean, how many vegetable shops are there in town? He started doing deliveries and packaging vegetables according to the needs of housewives. He was enormously successful. His family went through very difficult times, but they were committed. You can be committed to your dreams or plans, or you can just make a contribution. Remember the difference between a contribution and commitment the next time you have an egg for breakfast: the chicken made a contribution (egg) to your breakfast, while the pig made a commitment (bacon)—he died to be on your plate. Are you willing to die for your ideas, dreams or plans?

If you are in the debt spiral, you *can* escape from it. But it will be necessary to make serious commitments over a period of time. If you are on your own, it will be much easier to get out of the debt spiral. If you have a family, then you have to call a family meeting, discuss the issues with the whole family and make sure that everyone understands why you have a shortage on your income statement. Explain to the family that you need to pay your debts and therefore certain sacrifices have to be made to take you and the family through the difficult times. One day, after we had lost about R500 000 in a business deal and were facing a shortfall for the next 18 months, we sat and discuss how we were going to work through this difficult period and how every member of the family would have to take a cut in pocket money, that we would no longer go out for dinner on Friday evenings and would have to make some other sacrifices. After the discussions I walked to our bedroom, and the next moment my son of six (at that stage) said to me: "Dad, here is my R2 to help you with the down payment." I asked him whether that was the only money he had, and he said yes. Then I realised he understood that he was part of the family and also wanted to make his commitment. I took it, because I wanted him to know he belonged and that his sacrifice, however small, was appreciated. If your family understands, they will take on the challenge and you will become a strong team. Let everybody say what they think they will give up in the months to come and where they feel the rest of the family could save. When you share the recovery plan with them, they will know they are going to be exposed to a difficult period of 18 to 36 months, but after that things will get better, and then you know everybody shared the burden. Believe you me, nobody would like to have such an experience again, and you can rest assured money will be respected in future.

Compiling a financial wellness recovery plan

A budget is always important. The fact that I now concentrate on your recovery process does not mean I don't budget. A recovery plan is, in a sense, a budget as well. You will recognise the principles of budgeting we discussed in a previous chapter. After your recovery process has been completed, carry on planning, and spend your money in accordance with a budget.

I am going to focus more on the recovery plan. Although the approach might be a bit different, the principles of both the future financial wellness plan and the financial wellness recovery plan are the same.

This chapter must be read very closely together with the first chapter in this book, because the principles we discussed there should now be applied.

This is the heart and soul part. If you can grab this, you will not believe the change God will make in your life. And take my word for it: this is not difficult; you must have faith in yourself, focus and take control over your future!

In his book "The Richest Man of Babylon", George S. Clason tells the story of this person who became a slave because he didn't pay his debt. Just imagine, back in those days if you did not pay your debt, the creditor had the right to make you work for him as a slave. Being a slave wasn't easy those days; if you read books on slavery, you can hardly believe it. When he became a slave, he lost his self-image, family and the possibility to grow his own life. But then he met a man who explained to him what he had to do to get out of his misery. A principle that stands out in the advice that was given to him was the following:

- You must provide for your family and you must do it responsibly.
- You must pay your creditors.
- You must have access to cash and be able to manage it.
- Plan your work and work your plan

The principles of making and managing money are discussed in The Richest Man of Babylon, and training is done by the richest person in Babylon. Now if these principles worked in those years, why would they not work now?

I normally say to my children: your environment and technology may change, but good principles and manners never change. Even Barack Obama said in his inauguration speech that there are chances, but certain things are old and will stay forever. Corruption, stealing and cheating have existed as long as mankind exists. If you base your life on bad principles, it will fall apart. There is a saying that what you sow, you will reap. Stick to the basic good manners; is not difficult to say 'thank you' and 'please'.

Let's define the steps you need to take to recover from your in-debtedness.

Step 1: You must provide for your family and you must do it responsibly.

> **1 Timothy 5:8** *But if anyone does not provide for his relatives, and especially for members of his household, he has denied the faith and is worse than an unbeliever.*

The fact that you are in financial trouble and struggle to provide for your family is the first thing you must rectify. Get your family together and see what the absolute minimum expenditure is you will be able to survive on: no luxuries, just the essential expenses over a period of 24 months or longer. You will see in the case study of Mr Bru that we were able to get him out of the financial jail within 25 months.

Step 2: You must pay your creditors.

This is not negotiable. You will have to pay your creditors; this is a sound principle and good manners. Always pay your creditors.

Paying your creditors is part of honesty. I once spoke to a person who said he was not going to pay back the loan he had made because the person he had borrowed the money from was very rich and could do without the money he had lent him. In my book, that is stealing and definitely not fair play. Fair play is abiding by the rules of the game. There is a strong tendency among South Africans not to pay their debts. The consequences are that you can be placed under debt review or administration, and in an extreme case you can be declared insolvent (bankrupt). I have already discussed this as well as the consequences.

You may (and I recommend this) make appointments with your creditors and show them your recovery plan. You may negotiate a lower interest rate, a smaller instalment, a longer payback term or skipping one or two instalments, but you must never stop paying your creditors.

In the case study I will explain all the columns on the recovery sheet: your current instalment and the outstanding balance, the current payback term, your suggested payback term. You may reach an agreement with the creditor to pay the current instalments and agree on a payback plan for the arrears. The specimen document is a very adaptable document; you must change it so as to find the balance between what you can afford and what the creditor finds acceptable. Make sure you draw up a plan you will be able to carry out and stick to it. KEEP YOUR PROMISE!

Step 3: You must have access to cash and be able to manage it.

You obviously have your regular salary or wage, and you need to split it in such a manner that you meet all the expenses you have identified.

If you can increase your income, you can shorten your recovery period. Never make the mistake of spending your additional income on unplanned expenses. The whole purpose of the plan is to pay back all your creditors in the shortest time possible. If you achieve that, the creditors will always be willing to help you again in future.

Finding additional income can be very exciting. Always start with your employer; find out if there is any overtime or extra work that you can do for some extra income. Share with your employer your current financial crisis and your plan for getting out of it. If your employer cannot accommodate you with extra work, agree with your employer that you are going to explore other avenues for extra income, but also promise that it will not interfere with your current work output.

Where do you start with extra income? The best way is to see if you don't have a passion for something you can do that can earn you some extra income. My dad was a mechanic, and he worked for friends and family—private work, as he called it. He eventually opened his own garage, became owner of his own business and supplied employment to a number of people.

That means you must find creative ways to increase your income. Take on an after-hours job, start selling products and services, get your family involved in a business opportunity. Whenever you take on a business venture, make sure that you don't incur additional costs that put pressure on your income.

You can also generate cash by paying certain creditors a smaller amount in order to pay another creditor—not for you to spend on unplanned expenses. You will see in the case study how I make use of this principle.

Step 4: Plan your work and work your plan. When you draw up your recovery plan, you will see that it is going to be very challenging to implement it. You have to stick to the plan no matter what. You will remember that I described your position of indebtedness as being in financial jail, and getting out of jail is not easy. Be committed and be successful and free!

> **Matthew 17:20** *He said to them, "Because of your little faith. For truly, I say to you, if you have faith like a grain of mustard seed, you will say to this mountain, 'Move from here to there,' and it will move, and nothing will be impossible for you."*

I am going to make use of a case study to explain how you must compile your own recovery plan. If you follow the process, you will be able to do it yourself. If you need any of these forms, you can order them from hennier@pcd. co.za

Mr Bru was in trouble. Every month he just fell further and further behind in paying back his creditors. We followed certain rules and compiled a recovery plan for him.

Essential expenses

I explained to him that he had to provide for his family first, so he had to determine his essential expenses first (see table 3). So you write down those expenses you need to incur in order to support your family as well as the amount that you have to pay and in the column next to it what you think you will be able to afford. Fixed amounts, like rent for your house, can't be changed, therefore write the legally correct amount in the second column. Essential expenses are the absolute minimum you can live with!

Essential expenses: Table 3		
Item	Instalment or payment	Your committed instalment
House rent	4 000,00	4 000,00
Electricity	1 800,00	1 800,00
Transport	1 200,00	1 200,00
Groceries	1 800,00	1 450,00
School fees	1 500,00	1 500,00
Total essential expenses	**10 300,00**	**9 950,00**
Savings on essential expenses		350,00

You can see that by cutting back on the groceries, there is already a saving of R350,00.

The next step now is to list all the creditors you need to pay back. Table 4 shows how we list them.

Creditors Table 4			
Item	Outstanding balance	Instalment or payment	Remaining payback period
Woolworths	5000	500	10
Edgars	6000	600	10
Ackermans	3000	300	10
Wesbank	60000	3000	20

Capitec Bank	30000	2000	15
Corner Finance	20000	2500	8
Total creditors	**124000**	**8900**	

The monthly amount you need to pay the creditors is R8 900. The question is, do you have enough available to pay that every month? Let's now calculate what Mr Bru had available monthly.

Mr Bru's monthly income statement Table 5	
Essential expenses	10 300,00
Creditors payment	8 900,00
Total income needed	**19 200,00**
Minus current Income	15 000,00
Shortfall 1	**-4 200,00**
Minus saving on essential expenses	350,00
Shortfall 2	**-3 850,00**

The total income needed is R19 200. Mr Bru only has R15 000 available, which leaves him with a monthly shortfall of R4 200. He could save R350 on his essential expenses, so that means we must get him R3850 per month from somewhere. The solution is not to try to borrow this money; he must either explore some additional income opportunities—working overtime, doing some extra work or finding or making things that he can sell for extra income. Or he can try to reduce his expenses, and that is what I advise him to do. Extra income opportunities must always be explored, of course; if you can earn extra income and pay it into your recovery plan, you will be out of your debt spiral much sooner.

We are going to draft a recovery plan where we will able to schedule a meeting with the creditors and negotiate a settlement programme over a period of time with them. That will mean that we pay some of them less and others more.

There are a number of methods to determine the best kind of settlement for each creditor. The general principles are:

- Pay the creditors with the longest term a smaller amount initially and more later.
- Pay the creditors with the shortest period more to get them settled as quickly as possible.
- If you can settle the creditor with the highest interest fastest, it will save you a lot of money; therefore pay them more per month.
- Settle the creditors with the smallest outstanding amount quickest.
- Try to negotiate a longer term and a smaller instalment initially with some of the creditors, and then, as you pay the other creditors off, you increase these creditors' instalments, which will then shorten the payback period again.
- Remember, you will be guided by the creditor; but the creditor must also understand that you are willing to make a commitment to him, so he must also be lenient and accommodate you.

After we evaluated Mr Bru's creditors, we drew up a plan and we made sure that we had enough money available to break even on the income statement. We visited all his creditors, and they accepted his proposal. We listed the creditors as seen in Table 6 and set up a proposal for the first ten months.

Creditors payback plan for 10 months

Table 6

Name	Outstanding balance	Instalment or payment	Remaining payback period	Committed instalment	Time needed for payback	Difference in rand value	Difference in term
Woolworths	5 000,00	500,00	10	100,00	50	-400,00	40
Edgars	6 000,00	600,00	10	150,00	40	-450,00	30
Ackermans	3 000,00	300,00	10	300,00	10	—	0
Wesbank	60 000,00	3 000,00	20	2 500,00	24	-500,00	4
Capitec Bank	30 000,00	2 000,00	15	1 000,00	30	-1 000,00	15
Corner Finance	20 000,00	2 500,00	8	1 000,00	20	-1 500,00	12
Total creditors	124 000,00	8 900,00		5 050,00		-3 850,00	
Saving on creditors				3 850,00			

Mr Bru's income statement now looked as follows (see Table 7):

Mr Bru's monthly income statement Table 7	
Essential expenses	10 300,00
Creditors' payment	8 900,00
Total income needed	**19 200,00**
Minus current income	15 000,00
Shortfall 1	**-4 200,00**
Minus saving on essential expenses	350,00
Shortfall 2	**-3 850,00**
Minus savings on creditors	3 850,00
Breakeven (in balance)	Nil

In our 10-month plan, it looks as if we are going to pay the creditors back in as much as 50 months, which is more than 4 years. The period was actually shorter. We used the amount of R5 050 every month to pay the creditors. After 10 months one of the creditors (Ackermans) was fully paid, and we redistributed the funds available and paid identified creditors a bit more. After 20 months another 2 creditors were fully paid, namely Woolworths and Corner Finance. Then we redistributed the available funds again. See Table 8 for all these calculations.

Creditors detail Table 8

Name	Outstanding balance	Installment or payment	Outstanding payback period	Plan for the first 10 months — Your committed installment	Time needed for payback	Plan for the second 10 months — Your committed installment	Time needed for payback	Plan for the next 2 months — Your committed installment	Time needed for payback	Plan for the next 2 months — Your committed installment	Time needed for payback	Plan for the next month — Your committed installment	Time needed for payback
Woolworfhts	5000	500	10	100	50	400	10	0	0	0			
Edgars	6000	600	10	150	40	150	30	1500	2				
Ackermans	3000	300	10	300	10	0	0	0	0				
Wesbank	60000	3000	20	2500	24	2500	14	2550	3.92	2450	2		
Capitec Bank	30000	2000	15	1000	30	1000	20	1000	10	2600	3.08	2800	
Corner Finance	20000	2500	8	1000	20	1000	10	0	0	5050		5050	1
Total Creditors	124000	8900		5050		5050		5050		5050		2250	
The saving on creditors				3850						5050		5050	

The full creditor recovery plan is shown in Table 9. After 24 months, Mr Bru had an additional R2250, 00 in his pocket and in month 25 he had R5050,00. With this method it took him 25 months to clear all his debt. The main thing is that he stayed in control of his finances for this period, he paid nobody any fees etc. and the period of recovery was dramatically shorter.

True, life does not always go according to your plan. But if you hit a crisis, then you know where and how your plan needs to be changed to get you back on the road.

Creditors Settlement plan Table 9

Name	Outstanding balance	Payments made after 10 months	Balance after 10 months	Payments after 20 months	Balance after 20 months	Payments after 2 months	Balance after 22 months	Payments after 2 months	Balance after 24 months	Payments after 1 month	Balance after 25 months
Woolworths	5 000.00	1 000.00	4 000.00	4 000.00	—	—					
Edgars	6 000.00	1 500.00	4 500.00	1 500.00	3 000.00	3 000.00	—				
Ackermans	3 000.00	3 000.00	—	—	—		—				
Wesbank	60 000.00	25 000.00	35 000.00	25 000.00	10 000.00	5 100.00	4 900.00	4 900.00	—		
Capitec Bank	30 000.00	10 000.00	20 000.00	10 000.00	10 000.00	2 000.00	8 000.00	5 200.00	2 800.00	2 800.00	—
Corner Finance	20 000.00	10 000.00	10 000.00	10 000.00	—						
Total creditors	124000	50 500.00	73 500.00	50 500.00	23 000.00	10 100.00	12 900.00	10 100.00	2 800.00	2 800.00	NIL
Saving on creditors per month									2 250.00	5 050.00	
Duration of recovery plan		10 months		20 months		22 months		24 months		25 months	

CHAPTER 8

DEFINITIONS

> **Matthew 6:20** *But lay up for yourselves treasures in heaven, where neither moth nor rust destroys and where thieves do not break in and steal.*

I have not defined these financial concepts at a high academic level; I wanted to make sure they are practical and understandable.

There are many financial concepts, but I will explain only the basic ones. Most of these concepts were used in the book and defined there as well.

Work through these definitions and try to memorise them. They will help you in your day-to-day financial management.

Administration
In essence, being under administration means you appoint an attorney to manage your payments to your creditors.

The attorney will take a portion from your salary every month and pay it over to the creditors. You are responsible for all the fees. This can carry on for a very long period—5 to 10 years—and you are not allowed to make any debt during this period.

Cash flow

This is the amount of money you have available to pay your expenses and have available to buy yourself certain extras. You can have a positive cash flow, which means that after you have bought everything you need you still have money left. If you have a negative cash flow, it means that you need additional money to pay for all your expenses for the month. That's when your problems start, because now you have to borrow money from somebody to make ends meet. The moment you make a loan and you didn't plan it properly, you step into the debt cycle.

Debt cycle

The debt cycle can also be called a debt spiral. This spiral has a downward trend. That means that you will be worse off every month: your debt will become more and more every month, because of the interest that you have to pay and maybe additional shortfalls on certain expenses you can't meet. The fact that you are worse off every month creates emotions of unhappiness, fear, blame and conflict between you and your family members. There are cases where people have committed suicide or even killed the whole family, or totally destroyed the family relationship by divorce.

We have statistical proof that the debt cycle is a very dangerous situation to be in. Therefore, stay out of it in the first place. Be able to identify—and do be honest!—the signs that you are moving into this dangerous cycle. You will know when you are overindebted because you will simply have no money available to pay your expenses after you have paid for your basic living needs. In some cases, people find themselves in the situation that all the instalments are deducted from their salary through garnishee orders and they don't even have money left to buy food.

The principle with money is that you may not spend more than you have. Unfortunately, people compare themselves with others, see things on TV and want to show off to family and friends and then spend money on things they don't need. To stay out of debt, you need strict principles and methods. To get you out of your debt, you need a strategy.

Debt review
A debt review is done by a debt counsellor, who will investigate your situation and then takes control of your salary and pays off your creditors. You will not be allowed to make any debts until all accounts have been settled. Remember, the counsellor also takes his commission from your salary. You could use that amount of commission to help pay off your debt if you arrange your own recovery plan. So stay in control of you own finances.

Expenditure
This means all the money you spend, for whatever reason.

Fixed expenses

These are expenses that appear with the same amount every month. The amount might change from year to year (e.g. insurance premiums, medical scheme membership fees etc.). When you do your planning, you will know exactly what you need to pay on each item: instalments on your motor vehicle, rent for your house etc.

Gross monthly salary

This is the total amount you earn from your employer before any deductions.

Income

This is the amount (or amounts) flowing into your household. All money that 'comes in'.

Insolvent

You are insolvent if you are finally and completely unable to pay your debts, which are greater than the value of everything you possess. At this point all your assets are sold and the proceeds are used to pay your creditors. The shortfall will be written off by the creditors, and you will not be responsible for paying it back. You will not be allowed to make any debt for at least the next five years. After 5 years you go through a lengthy process to have yourself declared rehabilitated and fit to take up credit again.

In the cases of insolvency, administration and debt review, your name will be listed at the credit bureau. This is an organisation where all the persons who don't pay their bills are listed. The moment you apply for credit, a request will be launched with the bureau, and all the information on how you handle your accounts will be listed. There is also a list available of all credit that you have taken up with different institutions, with the specific details of each account such as the outstanding amount, initial loan amount, payment terms etc. All financial services must check if you can afford the loan. If you can't afford the loan and the loan is granted, the institution can be held responsible for reckless lending. Reckless lending can be very costly for the institution, because the law states that this debt, if proven, must be written off. As the borrower, you must always, whenever you fill in an application for credit, remember to declare all existing debts because they will be picked up through the National Credit Register. You can't disappear for a few years and try to come back into the system; it would not work, because your details will stay on the system for many a year.

Instalments
These are the amounts you pay off on any loan or credit—payments on your car, personal loans, clothing accounts etc.

Interest paid
When you have a loan from a bank, you will pay more money back to the bank than the initial capital you borrowed. This additional amount is called interest paid. Let's say you borrowed R1000 and they charge you 10% interest. You will then pay back to them the amount of R1100 [R1000 + (R1000*10%)]. Interest is an expense.

Interest received
When you make an investment with a bank or financial house, you will receive money on you investment, and that is called interest received. Let's say you made an

investment of R1000 and they offer you 10% interest per year, then you will earn R100 for the year. This is an income.

Loss
This is the amount you get if you deduct the expenses from your income and the amount is negative. That means your income is smaller than your expenses.

Net monthly salary
This is the amount that is paid out to you after deductions. You must make sure what is deducted from your salary. Only statutory deductions (tax, UIF etc.) are allowed.

Premiums
These are the monthly amounts you pay on your life insurance and short-term insurance policies.

Profit/surplus
This is the amount you get when you deduct the expenses from your income and you get a positive amount. That means your income is bigger than your expenses.

Variable expenses
These are expenses that fluctuate every month. Your electricity bill, for example, will be different every month. Always remember to check the variations on these expenses; they cannot be too large.

> **Isaiah 25:1-12** *O Lord, you are my God;*
> *I will exalt you; I will praise your name, for*
> *you have done wonderful things, plans formed*
> *of old, faithful and sure. For you have made*

the city a heap, the fortified city a ruin; the foreigners' palace is a city no more; it will never be rebuilt. Therefore strong peoples will glorify you; cities of ruthless nations will fear you. For you have been a stronghold to the poor, a stronghold to the needy in his distress, a shelter from the storm and a shade from the heat; for the breath of the ruthless is like a storm against a wall, like heat in a dry place. You subdue the noise of the foreigners; as heat by the shade of a cloud, so the song of the ruthless is put down . . .

www.ingramcontent.com/pod-product-compliance
Lightning Source LLC
Chambersburg PA
CBHW030906180526
45163CB00004B/1725